Klaus Heizmann

Vocal Warm-ups
200 Exercises for Choral and Solo Singers

With an introduction by
Simon Carrington

ED 9564

 SCHOTT

Mainz · London · Berlin · Madrid · New York · Paris · Prague · Tokyo · Toronto
© 2003 SCHOTT MUSIC GmbH & Co. KG, Mainz · Printed in Germany

Dedicated to
Victoria and Magnus

© 2003 Schott Music GmbH & Co. KG, Mainz
ISBN 978-3-7957-5259-0
ISMN 979-0-001-13397-5
Translation: Maryann Onofrietto, Anja Utsch
Voice training consultant: Lynne and Richard Ewert
Cover design: Dorothee Kraemer / H. J. Kropp
Illustrations: Sonja Wegener
Printed in Germany · BSS 50981

Contents

Introduction

When I retired from The King's Singers after my 25-year career, I had probably never sung a proper vocal warm-up in my life! Our idea in those days was to turn up for rehearsals or concerts having warmed up thoroughly on our own. As a teacher, it did not take me long to learn that this is wishful thinking. After ten years of teaching choirs, I have now used almost every warm-up technique known to man or woman!

Klaus Heizmann's collection is a wonderful new resource of ideas and techniques: practical, varied, challenging, relaxing and stimulating. I am always looking for new ideas, as I like to use a different set of warm-ups at every rehearsal with my choirs, and I tend to choose specific exercises to suit the repertoire for the day.

This collection gives us 200 excellent "tools-of the-trade"; they are clearly labeled, intelligently set out, well-designed and extremely useful. I can't wait for the new semester so that we can get to work stretching ourselves in all these new directions, physically, mentally and vocally.

Simon Carrington

Director of Choral Activities, New England Conservatory since 2001
Director of Choral Activities, The University of Kansas 1994-2001
Founder and co-director of The King's Singers 1968-1993

Preface

A chorus does not produce a balanced, homogeneous and natural sound automatically. It must learn to create this sound and develop an ear for it through targeted exercises. The purpose of choral voice training is not to provide singers with artistic singing instruction, but merely to give them the "tools" they need for fruitful collaboration in a chorus.

Fortunately, the importance of choral voice training has received increased recognition over the last few years. This publication is intended to provide chorus directors with a host of exercises to choose from. I collected them on the numerous trips I have taken to visit professional and amateur choruses in Germany and abroad. All chorus directors I consulted concerning this project had one thing in common: they were constantly in search of new and interesting warm-up exercises, because singing the same ones year in and year out results in lack of concentration and boredom. Consequently, I hope that these warm-up exercises can breathe some life back into chorus practice and make the singers curious about what their director will come up with for warming up at the next rehearsal.

The importance of these warm-up exercises must repeatedly be explained to singers. They are just as important as the warm-ups an athlete does before training or competition. Even if some individuals do not notice any great progress in the beginning, the small improvements each singer makes will considerably enhance the sound of the chorus as a whole. Signs of fatigue will become less frequent and the volume and sound of the chorus will gain intensity, homogeneity and versatility. Moreover, the voice will become stronger, smoother and more resilient. It is also important for a chorus director to work intensely on his own voice, experimenting with all of the suggested exercises several times himself first and using only those exercises he feels comfortable with when appearing in front of the chorus.

Because this book is also to be marketed internationally, conventional international notation is used: eighth-note beams instead of flags. The small guide notes that appear at the end of each warm-up exercise indicate how high and low the exercise should be sung. However, they are only suggestions and can be raised or lowered as needed. Similarly, all of the dynamic symbols are merely intended to provide guidelines and are not binding instructions.

The objectives of the warm-up exercises overlap in numerous instances. For example, an exercise for vowel modification is also good training for expanding vocal range or dynamics. Some of the exercises will inspire children's choruses to sing with great enthusiasm (e.g. 7.22), while eliciting only a tired grin from adults. Therefore, you should select the right combination of exercises for your special needs from this veritable treasure chest of experience collected from numerous choruses and soloists.

The human voice is the most sensitive and delicate of all instruments. Only with careful and responsible use over the years can it be kept healthy and strong. Choral voice training and these warm-up exercises can make a valuable and long-lasting contribution to achieving this goal.

Wiesbaden, Germany

Klaus Heizmann

Singing is the foundation of all music.
He who aims to compose must sing in his compositions.
He who plays instruments must be a master of song.
Thus, young people must be given thorough instruction in singing!

Georg Philipp Telemann
1681 – 1767

1. Physical warm-up exercises

After a long day at work or school, chorus members often come to practice tired. Some are tense, others feel exhausted.

The "posture" of some chorus singers

For this reason, warm-ups or voice training should always start with several relaxation exercises in order to prepare the chorus for singing and rehearsal.

The following exercises are intended to make singers aware of how damaging bad posture can be (see figure above) and demonstrate the posture that should be maintained when singing.

Although some singers might consider it childish to perform physical exercises, do not let this compromise your plans as chorus director. During my travels in countries outside Central Europe, I have often been surprised by the joyful and enthusiastic way physical exercises are performed at chorus rehearsals. We, more subdued, Central Europeans – particularly the older singers – have difficulty feeling natural and uninhibited during such exercises. Explain to your chorus that these exercises have the following goals, so that they will gradually come to understand how rewarding it is to participate:

- ♦ To create a cheerful atmosphere
- ♦ To loosen up and relax the entire body
- ♦ To promote body awareness
- ♦ To promote a feeling of well-being
- ♦ To increase awareness of diaphragmatic action and the breathing process
- ♦ To activate the resonance capacity of the body
- ♦ To illustrate the fact that music and motion belong together

Physical exercises should be performed in a relaxed atmosphere. The practice room should be well-ventilated, because having plenty of oxygen is important.

Basic position:

- ♦ Stand up straight with feet comfortably apart and firmly on the ground (see page 12)
- ♦ Let your arms hang loose at your sides
- ♦ Keep your back straight

Use images to describe the following exercises so that singers understand them properly. The instructions should be concise and illustrative.

Exercise 1   You are picking apples from a tree and placing them in a basket in front of you. Some of the apples are so high that you can only reach them by standing up on your toes and reaching as high as possible.
Or: You are lifting bricks onto scaffolding.
    You are hanging curtains.

Exercise 2   Stand on one leg, lift the other leg slightly and rotate your foot: first to the right a few times, then to the left. Switch legs and repeat.

Exercise 3   The singers massage each others backs and shoulders. Not too firmly!

Exercise 4   You are standing in front of the Eiffel Tower in Paris watching the elevator move slowly from the ground floor up to the top platform. After a brief pause, follow it back down again.

Exercise 5   You are on an opera stage receiving a round of applause from the audience. Take a deep bow, making sure your knees are slightly bent. Then stand up straight again to acknowledge the applause from the upper balconies. Your hands should be clasped behind your back.

Exercise 6   Lift your left shoulder up to your ear and hold the position briefly. Then let your arm and shoulder drop as if they were made of lead. Repeat with the right side. Breathe normally during this exercise, not in time with the raising and lowering of your shoulders.

Exercise 7 Slowly lower your head onto your right shoulder and hold the position briefly. Then swing it in a semicircle over your chest to the left shoulder, hold the position briefly and then return. Repeat about ten times.

Exercise 8 You are standing at the edge of a swimming pool in starting position for diving in. Your knees should be straight and whoever wants to can touch the floor or their toes with their hands.

Exercise 9 You are swinging an imaginary hula hoop around your hips. Both hands should be on the hips, the feet in fixed position.

Exercise 10 Stand like a stork. Bend your right leg and raise it as high as possible up to your stomach. Repeat four times and then switch legs.

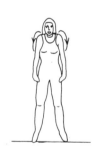

Exercise 11 Lift both shoulders and then let them drop loosely. Repeat about five times. Continue by rotating the left shoulder a few times and then the right. Finish by rotating both shoulders.

Exercise 12 This exercise should be part of every warm-up session. Have everyone yawn heartily and stretch all over. Then have them sigh several times from the highest to the lowest note. Shake out the arms.

2. The right posture

Try not to get tired of repeatedly reminding singers to maintain good posture, and also try to set a good example yourself. The right posture for sitting or standing is a basic prerequisite for good vocal performance.

♦ Stand as if you were balancing a basket of fruit on your head.
♦ Stand as if you were carrying a book on each shoulder.
♦ Each singer should stand as steadfastly as a lighthouse in a storm, rotating only the head from one side to the other like a beacon light.

Exercise:
Lean your back and especially your shoulders against a wall in such a way that you can feel the wall all over your back. Start with your feet about 20 cm in front of the wall and gradually slide them back to the wall.

The right standing posture:

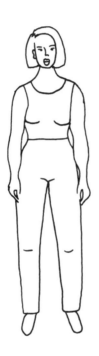

Feet comfortably apart
(shoulder width).

Knees not too stiff,
but rather relaxed and
flexible.

The wrong standing posture:

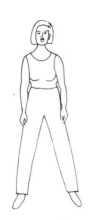  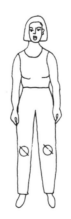 

1. Legs too far apart   2. Legs too close   3. Knees too stiff   4. Body weight on only
                                                                      one leg

The right sitting posture:

Sit up straight,
without leaning your
back on the backrest

Sit firmly on the
tailbone

Keep your feet flat
on the floor,
ready to stand up

Do not cross your legs
or fold your arms in front
of your chest

The wrong sitting posture:

1. Too far forward on
    the edge of the chair,
    back against the backrest

2. Back bent, legs
   under the chair

3. Legs crossed

g:

The right posture during a performance:

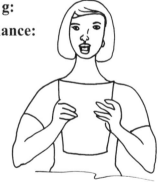

The wrong posture:

1. Tense

2. Neck area restricted

11

3. Model warm-up routines

Ten to fifteen minutes of warm-up and voice training are recommended prior to chorus practice. The following goals and tasks should be kept in mind:

♦ The purpose of the warm-up is to relax and limber up. Every runner takes a practice run to warm up before a 100-meter race – singers sing to warm up.

♦ Choral voice training can be combined effectively with warm-up exercises. It should not be a tiresome compulsory exercise, but rather an important part of responsible chorus training.

♦ A warmed-up voice ensures relaxed and less strenuous singing. There will be fewer signs of voice fatigue during chorus practice.

♦ The warm-up exercises should help singers learn "to hear themselves" and make them conscious of developing critical control over their own voice.

♦ Excessively forced, hard singing or screaming, should be prevented by the warm-up exercises, so that natural, clear singing can be achieved.

♦ Because every warm-up exercise uses intervals, singing them also promotes a good ear and thus clear intonation.

♦ The exercises can make singers aware of learning how to use uniform pronunciation and correct vowel formation.

♦ The warm-up exercises help to expand the vocal range and reach low and high notes effortlessly.

The following model routines are not an absolute standard, but rather serve as a general guideline. Moreover, the voice exercises should not be viewed as isolated elements. Their objectives overlap. For example, a dynamics exercise is also useful for expanding vocal range and for vowel modification. In order to get a brief overview, the exercises can be roughly divided into six different categories:

1. Physical warm-up exercises and posture
2. Breathing
3. Vocal warm-up exercises
4. Vowel formation and register transition
5. Resonance exercises
6. Combined exercises for intonation, expanding vocal range and developing a sense of rhythm

This sequence is not fixed. It should be tailored to the existing voices, the weaknesses of the singers and the music that is to be sung in the subsequent rehearsal or performance. Chorus directors should continually compile new warm-up routines for their own choruses, so that the singers do not become bored and distracted. However, proven exercises should form the basis of the warm-up. One thing should be kept in mind: when soprano, alto, tenor and bass singers warm up together, and not separately according to high and low voices, then the low voices should be asked to pause when the group is reaching for the higher notes, in order to avoid strain. Similarly, the high voices should not sing too deeply, because they then have a tendency to sing "from the chest" and lose the head tones.

The following models are not standards, but rather examples. They are representative of other exercises. For example, everyday voice training can begin with both of the following models and be modified later on.

Model 1

The chorus members should spread out in the room with plenty of space between them.

Physical warm-up exercises	1.1 – 1.2 – 1.4 – 1.12
Breathing exercises	4.1 – 4.9 – 4.12
Exercises for the diaphragm	5.1 – 5.6
Vocal warm-up exercises	7.1 – 7.4 – 7.16
Vowel formation/modification	8.6
Register transition	9.8
Ear training	13.1

The exercises can be concluded with a well-known canon that initially can be sung on one syllable (na, do, nu – depending on the nature of the composition). This can be followed by a familiar choral piece, so that the warm-up session leads right into the actual rehearsal.

Model 2

The chorus members should spread out in the room with plenty of space between them.

Physical warm-up exercises	1.2 – 1.6 – 1.9 – 1.11
Breathing exercises	4.2 – 4.3 – 4.5
Loosening/expanding the vocal tract	6.2 – 6.7
Vocal warm-up exercises	7.3 – 7.4 – 7.22
Vowel formation/modification	8.12
Lip warm-up	11.1
Ear training	13.3
Physical warm-up exercises	6.8

These exercises are followed by a well-known choral piece that initially can be sung on one syllable (na, no – depending on the nature of the composition).

4. Breathing exercises

It is beneficial to precede the actual warm-up exercises with a few, specific breathing exercises. They are performed in the basic position (see Chapter 2). Four basic rules should be observed in this context:

♦ Inhalation should never be audible or visible (do not raise the shoulders or rib cage during inhalation).
♦ Do not let the chest collapse during exhalation.
♦ Stand up straight, but generally keep the body relaxed.
♦ Do not fill the lungs "to the brim" with air, because it is not the volume of air that is decisive, but rather how you use it.

The following exercises generally have two different objectives:

♦ To promote calm and uniform air flow (Exercises 1 – 7).
♦ To activate the breathing muscles and the diaphragm (Exercises 8 – 14).

Breathing exercises

Exercise 1
Breathe primarily through the nose, without raising the chest or shoulders. Exhale on a soft **s** or **f**. Wait until you feel the urge to inhale, and then feel how the body breathes in on its own.

Exercise 2
Take three discontinuous breaths, as if you were smelling a flower. Simultaneously expand the pharynx. Then exhale three times. This effectively expands the nostrils, the back of the pharynx, the chest and the lower back, as they try to pass on the aroma to the body.

Exercise 3
Exhale by blowing out gently and uniformly. Imagine that you are:
♦ Blowing on a pinwheel
♦ Cooling hot soup
♦ Defrosting a frozen window pane

The breathing organs expand and the lung empties. Thoughts of these images are controlled by the central nervous system. Concentrating on them leads to increased muscular activity. In the region of the breathing muscles, this means more intense use of the inhalation cycle. Therefore, deliberately use images to lead the singers through these exercises.

Exercise 4
Exhale – pause – feel the urge to inhale – let the air slowly flow in again – exhale calmly and uniformly with a soft, silent **s**; do not sputter. Repeat the exercises with a voiced **v** or **s**, **sh**. Make sure that the throat is completely open and relaxed.

Exercise 5
Intense breathing: hold one nostril closed, inhale slowly and deeply through the other one and then exhale completely through the mouth. Alternate between the left and right nostril. During the exercise, feel the intake motion of the diaphragm, which is stronger now because it has to work harder to take in the same amount of air under these conditions.

Exercise 6
Exhale – pause – throat expanded – imitate an open "fish mouth" – wait until you feel the urge to inhale – let the air flow in and simultaneously be aware of your back muscles.

Exercise 7
Stand up straight. As you exhale, slowly bend your body forward until your hands almost touch the tips of your toes. Maintain this position until you stop exhaling. Then inhale and slowly straighten your upper body again. The region around the kidneys and below the last pair of ribs on the back will expand.

Exercises for activating the diaphragm

Exercise 8
Surprise breath, i.e. take one fast breath with the mouth open and a "surprised" facial expression. Simultaneously expand the mouth and pharynx region.

Exercise 9
Exhale with short, hard breaths. Imagine that:
♦ You have discovered some dust and want to blow it away with short, hard puffs.
♦ You are holding a withered dandelion in your hand and want to blow away the stubborn seeds with as few puffs as possible.

Exercise 10
♦ Inhale slowly, as if through a straw, and then exhale slowly through the straw.
♦ Exhale several times, like through the valve of a bicycle tire.

Exercise 11
The chorus singers imagine that they want to get a large, restless group of people to be quiet using the sound "**pssst**". However, since no one hears the warning **pssst** at first, the singers have to repeat it at different levels of intensity.

Exercise 12
Imitate an old steam train with the sound **tsh tsh tsh** ... Start up slowly – accelerate – decelerate. When you repeat the exercise, imagine how the puffs from the steam train become shorter as it gains speed and the volume decreases (*decrescendo*) as it moves farther away.

Exercise 13
Imitate a panting dog. Keep your chest still and let your "flanks" do the work. This exercise should not be performed too frequently, as it can easily cause dizziness.

Exercise 14
This exercise not only creates a positive, relaxed atmosphere but also loosens up tense muscles and activates the diaphragm. Have the chorus imitate various natural sounds, such as:

♦ A gentle evening breeze with a soft **f** (*piano*)
♦ A severe storm with **sh** (*forte* or *fortissimo*)
♦ An approaching and retreating swarm of bees with a soft **z** (*mezzoforte – crescendo – decrescendo*)

5. Exercises for deliberate diaphragmatic breathing

Breathing is primarily controlled by the diaphragm. Only correct and natural diaphragmatic breathing can provide the necessary support of the tone. Therefore, it is important for amateur singers first to become familiar with abdominal and diaphragmatic breathing by means of exercises. If a singer puts his hand on his stomach, he will feel how the diaphragm rises and falls. This kind of breathing must eventually become an unconscious habit. Just as a cellist deliberately adapts the movement of his bow to the phrase he is playing, a chorus singer must regulate and meter the flow of air by using the diaphragm correctly. Raising the shoulders while inhaling is generally not permitted, because it immediately leads to stiffening of the neck muscles and larynx. In addition, it does not provide sufficient breath support. Consequently, it is important to make singers repeatedly aware of the function of the diaphragm.

Exercise 1

Consonants should be unvoiced; start slowly and gradually accelerate.

Exercise 2

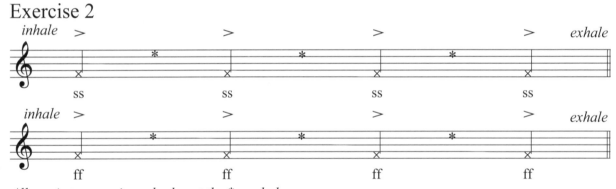

*Allow air to come in and relax at the * symbol.*
Be aware of the diaphragm, because it is the source of impulse, not the larynx.

Exercise 3

*Exhale at this point until you feel the urge to inhale. At the same time be aware of the diaphragm. You could place your hand on your stomach.

Exercise 4

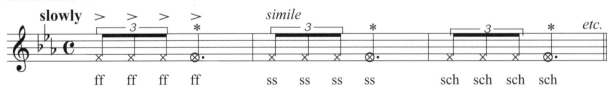

*See footnote to Exercise 3

Exercise 5

noo nun-ne nen-ne nahn noo nun-ne nen-ne nahn noo nun-ne nen-ne nahn

Let the diaphragm bounce at the accents.

Exercise 6

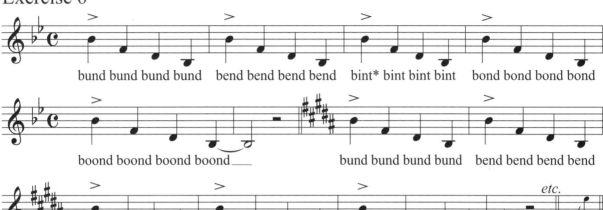

bund bund bund bund   bend bend bend bend   bint* bint bint bint   bond bond bond bond

boond boond boond boond____   bund bund bund bund   bend bend bend bend

bint* bint bint bint   bond bond bond bond   boond boond boond boond_

Let the diaphragm bounce at the accents.
* sounds like hint

Exercise 7

tah tah tah tah tah tah   tah tah tah   tah tah tah tah tah tah   tah tah tah

Exercise 8

hah   hah   hah   hah   hah   hah   hah   hah   hah

hah   hah   hah   hah   hah   hah   hah   hah   hah

Exercise 9

tah   tah   tah   tah   tah   tah   tah   tah   tah   tah   tah   tah

tah   tah   tah   tah   tah   tah   tah   tah   tah   tah   tah

tah   tah   tah   tah   tah   tah   tah   tah   tah   tah   tah

6. Exercises for relaxing and opening the vocal tract

While the function of the larynx can hardly be influenced at will, everything above it –the nose, mouth, throat and pharynx –can. Together, they are referred to as the vocal tract, which is like the funnel of an organ pipe. The vocal tract is responsible for forming sounds making use of the resonating cavities of the head. In order to create a good tone, the walls of the larynx must be elastic and loose, and the nose, mouth and pharynx must be expanded as much as possible.

Exercise 1

Exercises 1 to 6 help loosen up the vocal tract

Say the following syllables letting the lower jaw drop:

Additional syllables: vah vah vah, lah lah lah

Exercise 2

Exercise 3

Exercise 4

Say in a single breath:

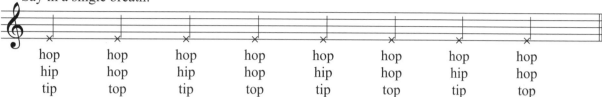

hop	hop	hop	hop	hop	hop	hop	hop
hip	hop	hip	hop	hip	hop	hip	hop
tip	top	tip	top	tip	top	tip	top

Exercise 5

Say in a single breath:

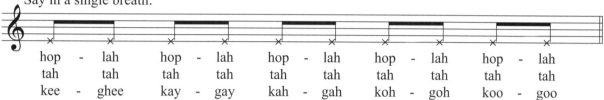

hop - lah	hop - lah	hop - lah	hop - lah	hop - lah
tah	tah	tah	tah	tah	tah	tah	tah
kee - ghee	kay - gay	kah - gah	koh - goh	koo - goo

Additional syllables: teedee tayday tahdah tohdo toodoo

Exercise 6

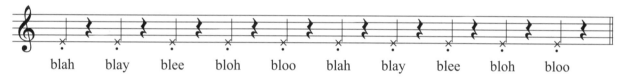

| blah | blay | blee | bloh | bloo | blah | blay | blee | bloh | bloo |

Exercise 7

Exercises 7 to 10 serve to expand the vocal tract

a.) Let the lower jaw drop as if it were filled with lead.
b.) Rotate the lower jaw with the mouth open.

Exercise 8

During rehearsal, have the chorus sigh frequently. Start as high as possible and gradually get lower. Sigh with the following vowels: oo, oh, ah

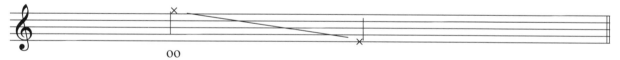

oo

Exercise 9

Say the following and let the chin drop at the same time:

oo

Exercise 10

Say the following:

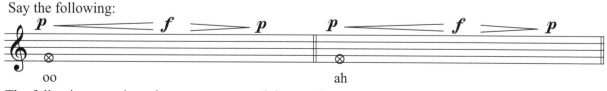

oo   ah

The following exercises also serve to expand the vocal tract:
4.2 (smelling a flower) and 4.8 (surprise breath with a surprised facial expression)

7. Vocal warm-up exercises

The lower jaw, which is generally only used to the strong, upward movement it makes when chewing, must be forced to execute relaxed downward movements, in order to create a sufficient amount of space. The tongue, which should be positioned behind the bottom teeth, must be relaxed. Stiff retraction and uncontrolled raising of the tongue considerably restrict the resonating cavity and make the vowels sound unnatural. Do not press your lips together; just let them come together gently. The following exercises not only loosen the lower jaw, tongue and lips, but also the entire vocal apparatus.

Exercise 1

Exercise 2

dah-bah dah-bah dah-bah dah-bah   dah-bah dah-bah dah-bah dah-bah   dah
doo-bee doo-bee doo-bee doo-bee   doo-bee doo-bee doo-bee doo-bee   doo
doh-boh doh-boh doh-boh doh-boh   doh-boh doh-boh doh-boh doh-boh   doh

Exercise 3

nah nah nah nah nah nah nah nah   nah nah nah nah nah nah nah nah   nah
noh noh noh noh noh noh noh noh   noh noh noh noh noh noh noh noh   noh
noo noo noo noo noo noo noo noo   noo noo noo noo noo noo noo noo   noo

nah nah nah nah nah nah nah nah   nah nah nah nah nah nah nah nah   nah
noh noh noh noh noh noh noh noh   noh noh noh noh noh noh noh noh   noh
noo noo noo noo noo noo noo noo   noo noo noo noo noo noo noo noo   noo

Exercise 4

blowblowblowblowblow blowblowblowblowblow blowblowblowblow blowblowblowblow
bly bly bly bly bly   bly bly bly bly bly   bly bly bly bly   bly bly bly bly

blow blow blow blow blow   blow blow blow blow blow   blow blow blow blow blow
bly bly bly bly bly   bly bly bly bly bly   bly bly bly bly bly

blow blow blow blow   blow blow blow blow   blow blow blow blow blow
bly bly bly bly   bly bly bly bly   bly bly bly bly bly

Additional syllables: blah, bloo

Exercise 5

yah yah yah yah yah yah yah yah   yah yah yah yah yah
yoo yoo yoo yoo yoo yoo yoo yoo   yoo yoo yoo yoo yoo
yoh yoh yoh yoh yoh yoh yoh yoh   yoh yoh yoh yoh yoh

yah yah yah yah yah yah yah yah   yah yah yah yah yah
yoo yoo yoo yoo yoo yoo yoo yoo   yoo yoo yoo yoo yoo
yoh yoh yoh yoh yoh yoh yoh yoh   yoh yoh yoh yoh yoh

Exercise 6

bah bah bah bah   beh beh beh beh   bee bee bee bee   boh boh boh boh___

bah bah bah bah beh beh beh beh bee bee bee bee boh boh boh boh___

Additional syllables:
bund bund bund bund bend bend bend bend bint* bint bint bint bond bond bond bond
* sounds like *hint*

Exercise 7

mah mee mah mee mah mee mah mee   mah mee mah mee mah
noh nee noh nee noh nee noh nee   noh nee noh nee noh
nah nee nah nee nah nee nah nee   nah nee nah nee nah

mah mee mah mee mah mee mah mee   mah mee mah mee mah
noh nee noh nee noh nee noh nee   noh nee noh nee noh
nah nee nah nee nah nee nah nee   nah nee nah nee nah

Additional syllables: mee mah, pea pah

Exercise 8

voh voh voh voh voh voh voh voh   voh_____
vah vah vah vah vah vah vah vah   vah_____
nee nee nee nee nee nee nee nee   nee_____

woh voh voh voh voh voh voh voh   voh_____
wah vah vah vah vah vah vah vah   vah_____
nee nee nee nee nee nee nee nee   nee_____

Additional syllables: noo, nay

Exercise 9

yah yah yah yah yah yah yah yah   yah yah yah yah yah
yay yay yay yay yay yay yay yay   yay yay yay yay yay
zoh zah zoh zah zoh zah zoh zah   zoh zah zoh zah zoh

yah yah yah yah yah yah yah yah   yah yah yah yah yah
yay yay yay yay yay yay yay yay   yay yay yay yay yay
zoh zah zoh zah zoh zah zoh zah   zoh zah zoh zah zoh

Exercise 10

noh
noo
nah

noh
noo
nah

Exercise 11

noh noh noh noh   noh noh noh noh   noh   noh noh noh noh   noh noh noh noh   noh
nah nah nah nah   nah nah nah nah   nah   nah nah nah nah   nah nah nah nah   nah
yoo yoo yoo yoo   yoo yoo yoo yoo   yoo   yoo yoo yoo yoo   yoo yoo yoo yoo   yoo

noh noh noh noh   noh noh noh noh   noh   noh noh noh noh   noh noh noh noh   noh
nah nah nah nah   nah nah nah nah   nah   nah nah nah nah   nah nah nah nah   nah
yoo yoo yoo yoo   yoo yoo yoo yoo   yoo   yoo yoo yoo yoo   yoo yoo yoo yoo   yoo

Additional syllables: zah, zee, nee

Exercise 12

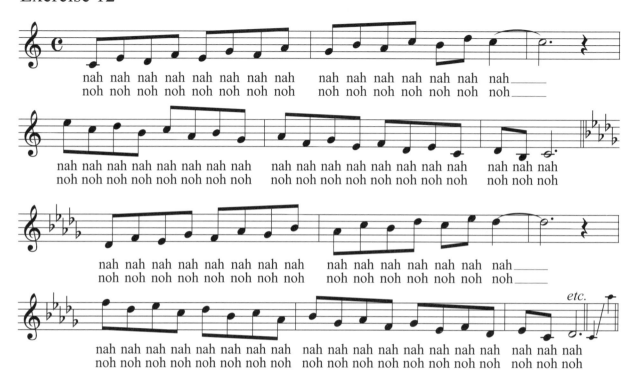

nah nah nah nah nah nah nah nah   nah nah nah nah nah nah nah_____
noh noh noh noh noh noh noh noh   noh noh noh noh noh noh noh_____

nah nah nah nah nah nah nah nah   nah nah nah nah nah nah nah nah   nah nah nah
noh noh noh noh noh noh noh noh   noh noh noh noh noh noh noh noh   noh noh noh

nah nah nah nah nah nah nah nah   nah nah nah nah nah nah nah_____
noh noh noh noh noh noh noh noh   noh noh noh noh noh noh noh_____

etc.

nah nah nah nah nah nah nah nah   nah nah nah nah nah nah nah nah   nah nah nah
noh noh noh noh noh noh noh noh   noh noh noh noh noh noh noh noh   noh noh noh

Exercise 13

doo - - - na doo - na   doo - na doo - na   doo - na
do - - - na do - na   do - na do - na   do - na
da - - - na da - na   da - na da - na   da - na

etc.

doo - - - na doo - na   doo - na doo - na   doo - na
do - - - na do - na   do - na do - na   do - na
da - - - na da - na   da - na da - na   da - na

Exercise 14

p ⎯⎯⎯⎯ *f* *p*

zah zah zah zah zah zah   zah zah zah zah_____   zah_____
noh noh noh noh noh noh   noh noh noh noh_____   noh_____
yoo yoo yoo yoo yoo yoo   yoo yoo yoo yoo_____   yoo_____

p ⎯⎯⎯⎯ *f* *p* *etc.*

zah zah zah zah zah zah   zah zah zah zah_____   zah_____
noh noh noh noh noh noh   noh noh noh noh_____   noh_____
yoo yoo yoo yoo yoo yoo   yoo yoo yoo yoo_____   yoo_____

Exercise 15

moh moh moh moh moh moh moh moh
moo moo moo moo moo moo moo moo

moh moh moh moh moh moh moh moh
moo moo moo moo moo moo moo moo

moh moh moh moh moh
moo moo moo moo moo

moh moh moh moh moh moh moh moh
moo moo moo moo moo moo moo moo

moh moh moh moh moh moh moh moh
moo moo moo moo moo moo moo moo

moh moh moh moh moh
moo moo moo moo moo

Additional syllables: mam, mum, nom, num

Exercise 16

f hah hah hah   hah hah hah   hah hah hah

hah hah hah   hah hah hah   hah hah hah

This exercise can also be sung from a lower tone rising chromatically.

Exercise 17

nah___ nah___ nah___   nah___ nah___ nah___   nah
noh___ noh___ noh___   noh___ noh___ noh___   noh
nee___ nee___ nee___   nee___ nee___ nee___   nee

nah___ nah___ nah___   nah___ nah___ nah___   nah
noh___ noh___ noh___   noh___ noh___ noh___   noh
nee___ nee___ nee___   nee___ nee___ nee___   nee

Exercise 18

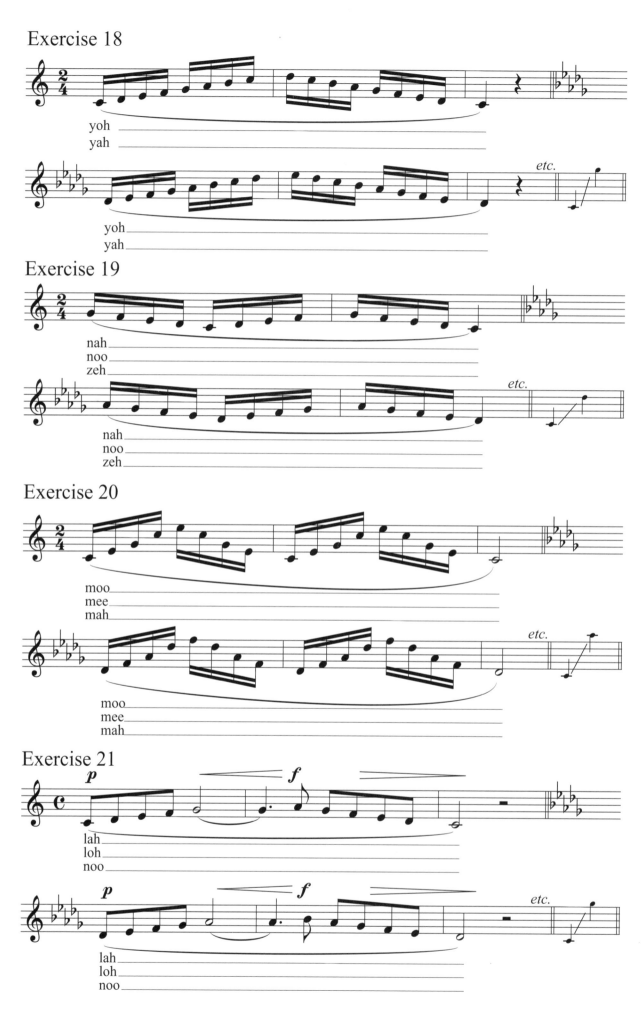

yoh

yah

yoh

yah

Exercise 19

nah

noo

zeh

nah

noo

zeh

Exercise 20

moo

mee

mah

moo

mee

mah

Exercise 21

lah

loh

noo

lah

loh

noo

Exercise 22

din-ga dong dong dong din-ga dong dong dong din-ga din-ga din-ga din-ga din-ga
Sing a song song song, sing a song song song, sing an it-ty-bit-ty, wit-ty, pret-ty

dong dong dong dah dee ding ding ding dah dee ding ding ding dah di
song song song. Sing a song song song, sing a song song song, sing an

dah dee dah dee dah dee dah dee ding ding ding din-ga dong dong dong din-ga
it-ty-bit-ty, wit-ty, pret-ty song song song. Sing a song song song, sing a

dong dong dong din-ga din-ga din-ga din-ga din-ga dong dong dong dah dee
song song song, sing an it-ty-bit-ty, wit-ty, pret-ty song song song. Sing a

etc.

ding ding ding dah dee ding ding ding dah dee dah dee dah dee dah dee ding ding ding
song song song, sing a song song song, sing an it-ty-bit-ty, wit-ty, pret-ty song song song.

Exercise for relaxation and ear training. Inwardly "hear" the new key before singing it.

Exercise 23

nah nah nah nah nah nah nah nah nah nah nah nah nah nah
noh noh noh noh noh noh noh noh noh noh noh noh noh noh

nah nah nah nah nah nah nah nah nah nah nah nah nah nah
noh noh noh noh noh noh noh noh noh noh noh noh noh noh

Exercise 24

p — *f*   *down or up*

mee - nah mee-nah mee-nah mee nah mee - nah
mee - ah mee-ah mee -ah mee-ah mee - ah

Exercise 25

nah nah nah nah nah nah nah nah nah nah nah nah nah nah nah nah   nah

nah nah nah nah nah nah nah nah nah nah nah nah nah nah nah nah nah

Exercise 26

hah   hah   hah   hah   hah   hah   hah   hah   hah   hah

hah   hah   hah   hah   hah   hah   hah   hah   hah   hah

Exercise 27

The con-so-nants should   be quite short, but   vow-els need to be   held out.

Exercise 28

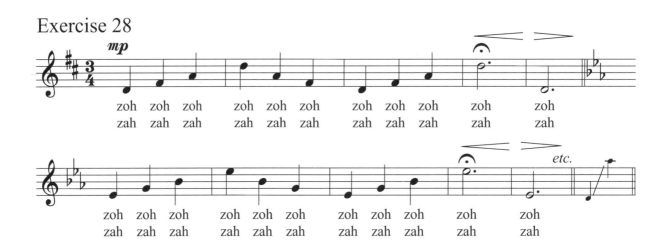

zoh zoh zoh   zoh zoh zoh   zoh zoh zoh   zoh   zoh
zah zah zah   zah zah zah   zah zah zah   zah   zah

zoh zoh zoh   zoh zoh zoh   zoh zoh zoh   zoh   zoh
zah zah zah   zah zah zah   zah zah zah   zah   zah

Exercise 29

zoh zoh zoh zah zoh zoh zoh zah
yay yay yay yah yay yay yay yah

etc.

zoh zoh zoh zah zoh zoh zoh zah
yay yay yay yah yay yay yay yah

Exercise 30

nah nah nah nah nah nah nah nah nah nah nah nah nah nah nah nah nah nah
yay yay yay yay yay yay yay yay yay yay yay yay yay yay yay yay yay yay
noo noo noo noo noo noo noo noo noo noo noo noo noo noo noo noo noo noo

nah nah nah nah nah nah nah nah nah nah nah nah nah nah nah nah nah nah
yay yay yay yay yay yay yay yay yay yay yay yay yay yay yay yay yay yay
noo noo noo noo noo noo noo noo noo noo noo noo noo noo noo noo noo noo

Exercise 31

etc.

zah zoh zah zoh   zah zoh zah   zah zoh zah zoh   zah zoh zah
zoh zah zoh zah   zoh zah zoh   zoh zah zoh zah   zoh zah zoh

Exercise 32

etc.

yoo yah yoo yah   yoo yah yoo   yoo yah yoo yah   yoo yah yoo
vee zoh vee zoh   vee zoh vee   vee zoh vee zoh   vee zoh vee

Exercise 33

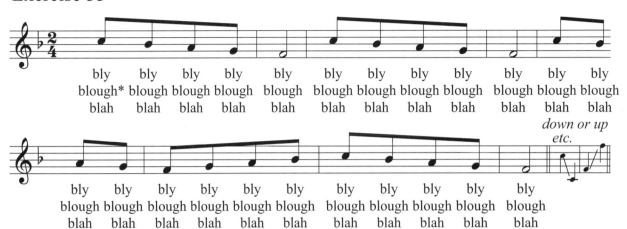

bly · bly · bly · bly · bly · bly · bly · bly · bly · bly · bly · bly
blough* blough blough blough · blough · blough blough blough blough · blough blough blough
blah · blah · blah · blah · blah · blah · blah · blah · blah · blah · blah · blah

down or up
etc.

bly · bly · bly · bly · bly · bly · bly · bly · bly · bly · bly
blough blough blough blough blough blough · blough blough blough blough · blough
blah · blah · blah · blah · blah · blah · blah · blah · blah · blah · blah

sounds like "now, cow"

Exercise 34*

yoh yoh yoh yoh yoh yoh yoh yoh · yoh · yoh yoh yoh yoh yoh yoh yoh yoh · yoh
yah yah yah yah yah yah yah yah · yah · yah yah yah yah yah yah yah yah · yah

etc.

Keyboard accompaniment for this exercise: Page 64

Exercise 35

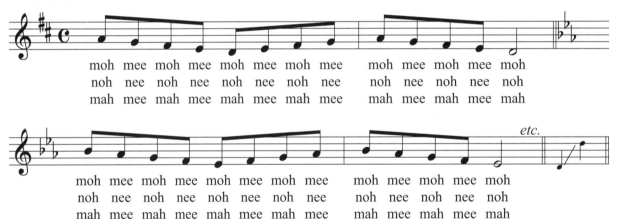

moh mee moh mee moh mee moh mee · moh mee moh mee moh
noh nee noh nee noh nee noh nee · noh nee noh nee noh
mah mee mah mee mah mee mah mee · mah mee mah mee mah

etc.

moh mee moh mee moh mee moh mee · moh mee moh mee moh
noh nee noh nee noh nee noh nee · noh nee noh nee noh
mah mee mah mee mah mee mah mee · mah mee mah mee mah

Exercise 36

noh noh noh noh noh noh noh noh · noh noh noh noh noh noh noh noh · noh
nah nah nah nah nah nah nah nah · nah nah nah nah nah nah nah nah · nah
noo noo noo noo noo noo noo noo · noo noo noo noo noo noo noo noo · noo

etc.

noh noh noh noh noh noh noh noh · noh noh noh noh noh noh noh noh · noh
nah nah nah nah nah nah nah nah · nah nah nah nah nah nah nah nah · nah
noo noo noo noo noo noo noo noo · noo noo noo noo noo noo noo noo · noo

Exercise 37*

mah mah mah mah mah mah mah mah   mah mah mah mah mah mah mah mah

mah mah mah mah mah mah mah mah   mah mah mah mah mah ma mah mah

mah mah mah mah mah mah mah mah   mah mah mah mah mah mah mah mah   mah

Known among singers as the "Caruso exercise"

Exercise 38

vah vah vah vah vah vah vah vah vah vah vah vahvah vah vah vah vah vah vah vah vah vah vah vah
vay vay vay vay vay vay vay vay vay vay vay vayvay vay vay vay vay vay vay vay vay vay vay vay
*ma-la- ga ma-la - ga ma-la - ga ma-la - ga ma-la - ga ma-la - ga ma-la - ga ma-la - ga

vah vah vah___   vah vah vah vah vah vah vah vah vah vah vah vah
vay vay vay___   vay vay vay vay vay vay vay vay vay vay vay vay
ma - la - ga___   ma - la - ga ma - la - ga ma - la - ga ma - la - ga

etc.

vah vah vah vah vah vah vah vah vah vah vah vah   vah vah vah___
vay vay vay vay vay vay vay vay vay vay vay vay   vay vay vay___
ma - la - ga ma - la - ga ma - la - ga ma - la - ga   ma - la - ga___

*Pronounce all a's like in *"car"*.

Exercise 39

mah___   mah___
mee___   mee___
moh___   moh___

etc.

mah___   mah___
mee___   mee___
moh___   moh___

Exercise 40

nah nah nah nah nah nah nah nah nah   nah nah nah nah nah nah nah nah nah
doh doh doh doh doh doh doh doh doh   doh doh doh doh doh doh doh doh doh
yah yah yah yah yah yah yah yah yah   yah yah yah yah yah yah yah yah yah

Exercise 41

nah nah nah nah nah nah nah nah nah nah nah nah nah nah   nah
doh doh doh doh doh doh doh doh doh doh doh doh doh doh   doh

nah nah nah nah nah nah nah nah nah nah nah nah nah nah   nah
doh doh doh doh doh doh doh doh doh doh doh doh doh doh   doh

Exercise 42

noh_____ noh
nah_____ nah
noo_____ noo

noh_____ noh
nah_____ nah
noo_____ noo

Exercise 43

ah_____ oh___ ah_____ oh___ ah
oo_____ ee___ oo_____ ee___ oo

ah_____ oh___ ah_____ oh___ ah
oo_____ ee___ oo_____ ee___ oo

nah nah nah nah nah nah nah nah nah nah nah nah nah nah nah nah   nah
noh noh noh noh noh noh noh noh noh noh noh noh noh noh noh noh   noh

etc.

nah nah nah nah nah nah nah nah nah nah nah nah nah nah nah nah   nah
noh noh noh noh noh noh noh noh noh noh noh noh noh noh noh noh   noh

Exercise 45

nah nah nah nah nah nah nah nah nah nah nah nah nah nah nah nah   nah nah nah nah
noh noh noh noh noh noh noh noh noh noh noh noh noh noh noh noh   noh noh noh noh

nah nah nah nah nah   nah nah nah nah nah nah nah nah
noh noh noh noh noh   noh noh noh noh noh noh noh noh

etc.

nah nah nah nah nah nah nah nah nah nah nah nah nah nah nah   nah
noh noh noh noh noh noh noh noh noh noh noh noh noh noh noh   noh

Exercise 46

nah_____
noh_____
noo_____

etc.

nah_____
noh_____
noo_____

Exercise 47

nah nah nah nah nah nah nah nah nah nah nah nah nah nah nah nah

nah nah nah nah nah nah nah nah nah   nah nah nah nah nah nah nah nah

etc.

nah nah nah nah nah nah nah nah nah nah nah nah nah nah nah nah   nah

8. Exercises for vowel formation and modification

A singer can form the different vowels by correctly positioning the tongue, lips and mouth and utilizing the resonating cavities of the head and chest. Because these vowels have very different tone colors, it is necessary to balance them out somewhat when changing from one vowel to another. For example, a dark "oo" should not be followed by an "ee" or "eh" sung too brightly. This is called vowel modification. The transition between vowels should be executed deliberately by changing the resonating cavity inside the mouth. The tone for all vowel sounds should be directed towards the front and into the head cavities.

Exercise 1

This exercise can also be sung at a faster tempo in a single breath.

Exercise 2

Exercise 3

oo ee oo ee oo ee oo ee oo ee oo ee oo
oh oo oh oo oh oo oh oo oh oo oh oo oh
oh ah oh ah oh ah oh ah oh ah oh ah oh

Exercise 4

a) Both measures in one breath
b) Breathe at the end of each measure

oo ee oo ee oo oo ee oo ee oo
oh ah oh ah oh oh ah oh ah oh

oo ee oo ee oo oo ee oo ee oo
oh ah oh ah oh oh ah oh ah oh

Exercise 5

mah nah lah_____
yoh moh noh_____
zoo too shoo_____

mah nah lah_____
yoh moh noh_____
zoo too shoo_____

Exercise 6

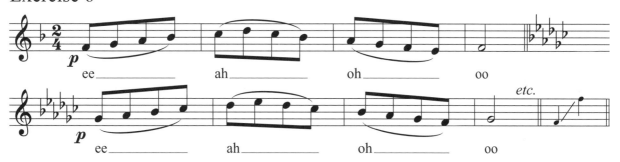

ee_____ ah_____ oh_____ oo

ee_____ ah_____ oh_____ oo

Exercise 7

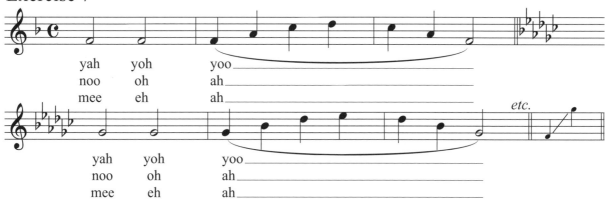

yah yoh yoo_____
noo oh ah_____
mee eh ah_____

yah yoh yoo_____
noo oh ah_____
mee eh ah_____

Exercise 8

ee___ ay ah___ oh___ oo

ee___ ay ah___ oh___ oo

Exercise 9

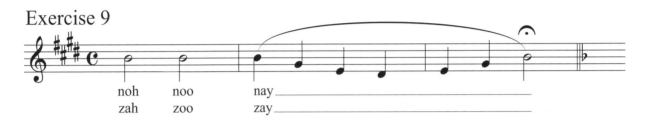

noh noo nay___
zah zoo zay___

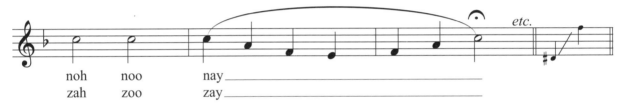

noh noo nay___
zah zoo zay___

Exercise 10

bly blough* bloy___
mah moh moo___

*sounds like *"now, cow"*

Exercise 11

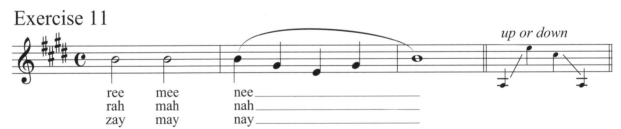

ree mee nee___
rah mah nah___
zay may nay___

Additional syllables: ngah, ngay, ngee

Exercise 12*

oo___ oh___ ah___

oo___ oh___ ah___

Keyboard accompaniment for this exercise: Page 65

Exercise 13

nahm naym neem nohm   nahm naym neem nohm   nahm naym neem nohm   nahm

nahm naym neem nohm   nahm naym neem nohm   nahm naym neem nohm   nahm

Sing slowly at first, then gradually faster.

Exercise 14

nah   nah   nah   nah   nah_____
noh   noh   noh   noh   noh_____

nah   nah   nah   nah   nah_____
noh   noh   noh   noh   noh_____

Exercise 15

nah nah nah nah   nah nah nah nah nah nah nah nah   nah
noh noh noh noh   noh noh noh noh noh noh noh noh   noh

nah nah nah nah   nah nah nah nah nah nah nah nah   nah
noh noh noh noh   noh noh noh noh noh noh noh noh   noh

Exercise 16

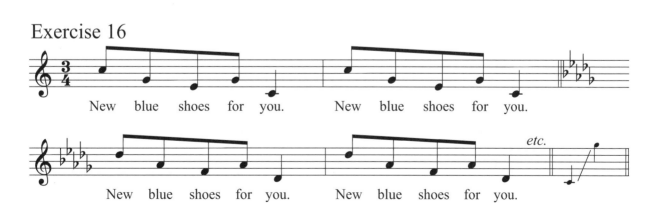

New   blue   shoes   for   you.   New   blue   shoes   for   you.

New   blue   shoes   for   you.   New   blue   shoes   for   you.

Exercise 17

See the sim-ple Si-mon sit-ting   still up-on the sill a-wait-ing   pies.

etc.

See the sim-ple Si-mon sit-ting   still up-on the sill a-wait-ing   pies.

Exercise 18

noh - ah noh - ah noh - ah noh - ah   noh - ah

etc.

noh - ah noh - ah noh - ah noh - ah   noh - ah

Exercise 19

ah_____ ay_____ ee_____ oh_____ oo_____

etc.

ah_____ ay_____ ee_____ oh_____ oo_____

Exercise 20

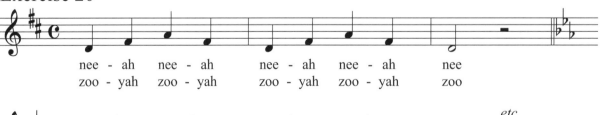

nee - ah nee - ah   nee - ah nee - ah   nee
zoo - yah zoo - yah   zoo - yah zoo - yah   zoo

etc.

nee - ah nee - ah   nee - ah nee - ah   nee
zoo - yah zoo - yah   zoo - yah zoo - yah   zoo

Exercise 21

may may may may mah_____ may may may may mah_____

Exercise 22

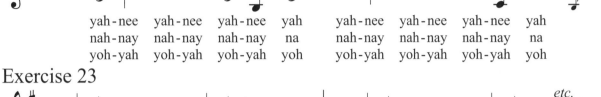

yah-nee yah-nee yah-nee yah yah-nee yah-nee yah-nee yah
nah-nay nah-nay nah-nay na nah-nay nah-nay nah-nay na
yoh-yah yoh-yah yoh-yah yoh yoh-yah yoh-yah yoh-yah yoh

Exercise 23

vah vay vee voh voo vah vay vee voh voo vah vay vee voh voo vah vay vee voh voo

Exercise 24

vah vay vee voh voo vah vay vee voh voo vah vay vee voo

vah vay vee voh vah vay vee voh voo vah vay vee voh voo

vah vay vee voh voo vah vay vee voo vah vay vee voh vah vay vee voh voo

Exercise 25

yoo yoh yah yoo yoh yah yoo yah yoh yoo yoh yah yoo yoh yah yoo yah yoh

Exercise 26

dah - boo dah - boo da - boo da - boo da - boo____
moh - nah moh - nah moh - nah moh - nah mo - nah____
meh - noh meh - noh meh - noh meh - noh meh - noh____

dah - boo dah - boo da - boo da - boo da - boo____
moh - nah moh - nah moh - nah moh - nah mo - nah____
meh - noh meh - noh meh - noh meh - noh meh - noh____

Exercise 27

yoo yoh yah yoo yoh yah   yoo yoh yah yoo yoh yah   yoo yoh yah yoo yoh yah   yoo

yoo yoh yah yoo yoh yah   yoo yoh yah yoo yoh yah   yoo yoh yah yoo yoh yah   yoo

Additional syllables: nee nay nah, noh nah nee

Exercise 28

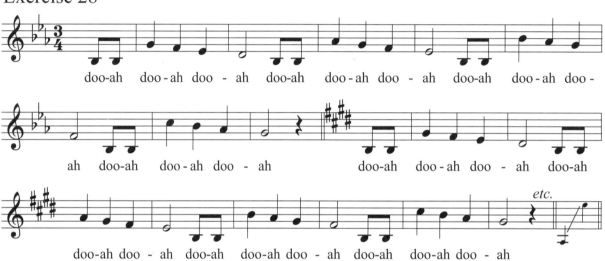

doo-ah   doo-ah   doo - ah   doo-ah   doo - ah doo - ah   doo-ah   doo - ah doo -

ah   doo-ah   doo - ah doo - ah   doo-ah   doo - ah doo - ah   doo-ah

doo-ah doo - ah   doo-ah   doo-ah doo - ah   doo-ah   doo-ah doo - ah

Exercise 29

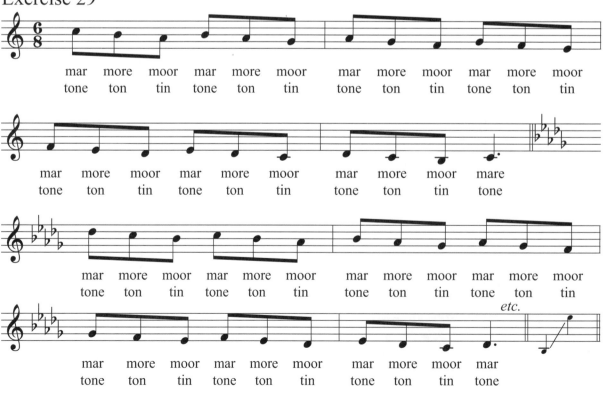

mar   more   moor   mar   more   moor   mar   more   moor   mar   more   moor
tone   ton   tin   tone   ton   tin   tone   ton   tin   tone   ton   tin

mar   more   moor   mar   more   moor   mar   more   moor   mare
tone   ton   tin   tone   ton   tin   tone   ton   tin   tone

mar   more   moor   mar   more   moor   mar   more   moor   mar   more   moor
tone   ton   tin   tone   ton   tin   tone   ton   tin   tone   ton   tin

mar   more   moor   mar   more   moor   mar   more   moor   mar
tone   ton   tin   tone   ton   tin   tone   ton   tin   tone

Exercise 30

noh noh noh noh___ noh noh noh noh___ noh noh noh noh___ noh noh noh noh___

noh noh noh noh___ noh noh noh noh___ noh noh noh noh___ noh

Exercise 31

noo mee noo mee noo mee noo mee noo

noo mee noo mee noo mee noo mee noo *etc.*

Exercise 32

may_____ mah_____ moh_____

may_____ mah_____ moh_____ *etc.*

Exercise 33

after Pauline Viardot-Garcia 1821-1910

ah___ oh___ ah___ oh___ ah___ oh___

ah___ oh___ ah___ oh___ ah___ oh___ ah___ oh___

ah___ oh___ ah___ oh___ ah___ oh___ ah

9. Register transition exercises

A singer's vocal range must be expanded in both directions so that the sound of the voice does not "break" when moving into different registers. The voice should not suddenly sound different beyond a certain pitch. Only with long-term, regular and expert voice training it is possible to develop a balanced voice, free of disturbing "breaks". The following exercises should be used for this purpose.

Exercise 1

nee-ah nee-ah nee-ah nee-ah nee-ah nee-ah nee-ah___
lah-oo lah-oo lah-oo lah-oo lah-oo lah-oo lah-oo___
may-oh may-oh may-oh may-oh may-oh may-oh may-oh___

nee-ah nee-ah nee-ah nee-ah nee-ah nee-ah nee-ah___
lah-oo lah-oo lah-oo lah-oo lah-oo lah-oo lah-oo___
may-oh may-oh may-oh may-oh may-oh may-oh may-oh___

Exercise 2

oo_____ oo_____
oh_____ oh_____
ah_____ ah_____

oo_____ oo_____
oh_____ oh_____
ah_____ ah_____

Exercise 3

oo_____
oh_____
ah_____

oo_____
oh_____
ah_____

Exercise 4

noh
ah
noo
may

noh
ah
noo
may

Exercise 5

oo
oh
ay

oo
oh
ay

Exercise 6

ah
oh
oo

ah
oh
oo

Exercise 7

Exercise 8

Exercise 9

Exercise 10

noh _____ noh
noo _____ noo
nah _____ nah

noh _____ noh
noo _____ noo
nah _____ nah

noh _____ noh
noo _____ noo
nah _____ nah

noh _____ noh
noo _____ noo
nah _____ nah

Exercise 11

zoh _____ zoh _____ zoh _____ *etc.*
zah _____ zah _____ zah _____

Exercise 12

moh-mee moh-mee moh-mee moh-mee   moh-mee moh-mee moh-mee moh-mee

moh-mee moh-mee moh-mee moh-mee   moh   moh-mee moh-mee moh-mee moh-mee

moh-mee moh-mee moh-mee moh-mee   moh-mee moh-mee moh-mee moh-mee   moh

10. Resonance exercises

Everyone has resonating cavities in their body and singers need to exploit these to the fullest. Good resonance requires the vibrations to be transmitted to all vibratory parts of the body, namely the nose, sinuses, mouth, pharynx, throat, tympanum, eye sockets and chest cavity. This not only enhances tone, but is also responsible for the unique, characteristic timbre of each person's voice. When singing loudly, the walls of the vocal tract and the resonating cavities should be relaxed. There should be no pressure on the throat. The best method for gaining volume is to first sing the exercises *piano* and then gradually increase the dynamics.

L, m, n, ng and v are good resonators.

With "ng": keep the mouth wide open, as with "a".

With "n": the tip of the tongue should rest lightly against the hard palate (not pressed).

Exercise 1

Exercise 2

Exercise 3

Additional syllable: nee
all vowels

Exercise 4

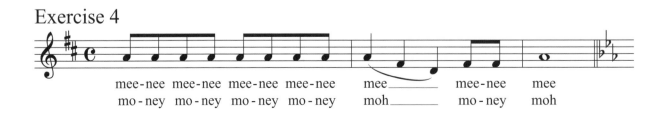

mee-nee mee-nee mee-nee mee-nee mee_____ mee-nee mee
mo-ney mo-ney mo-ney mo-ney moh_____ mo-ney moh

Exercise 5

m_____
n_____
ng_____

m_____
n_____
ng_____

Exercise 6

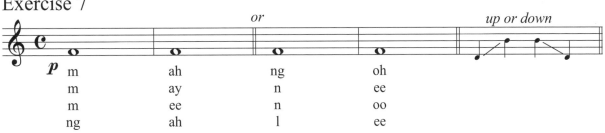

ng_____ ng_____
m_____ m_____
n_____ n_____

Exercise 7

or *up or down*

p m ah ng oh
m ay n ee
m ee n oo
ng ah l ee

Exercise 8

p
n___ oh_____ n___ oh_____
m___ ah_____ m___ ah_____
ng___ eh_____ ng___ eh_____

Exercise 9

n_____ z_____ n_____ z_____
m_____ z_____ m_____ z_____
m_____ oh_____ m_____ oh_____

Additional syllables: ng-ah

Exercise 10

nah-men nen-nen   nah-men nen-nen   nah-men nen-nen   nah-men nen-nen
non-nen nen-nen   non-nen nen-nen   non-nen nen-nen   non-nen nen-nen

Exercise 11

ding - a dong - a   ding - a dong - a   ding ding   ding

ding - a dong - a   ding - a dong - a   ding ding   ding

Exercise 12

nah nah nah nah nah nah nah   nah nah nah nah nah nah nah   nah
doh doh doh doh doh doh doh   doh doh doh doh doh doh doh   doh

nah nah nah nah nah nah nah   nah nah nah nah nah nah nah   nah
doh doh doh doh doh doh doh   doh doh doh doh doh doh doh   doh

Exercise 13

ming - a mang - a meng - a   mong mong mong   ming - a mang - a meng - a

mong mong mong   ming - a mang - a meng - a   mong mong mong

Exercise 14

noo noo noo noo noo noo noo noo   noo noo noo

noo noo noo noo noo noo noo noo   noo noo noo

Exercise 15

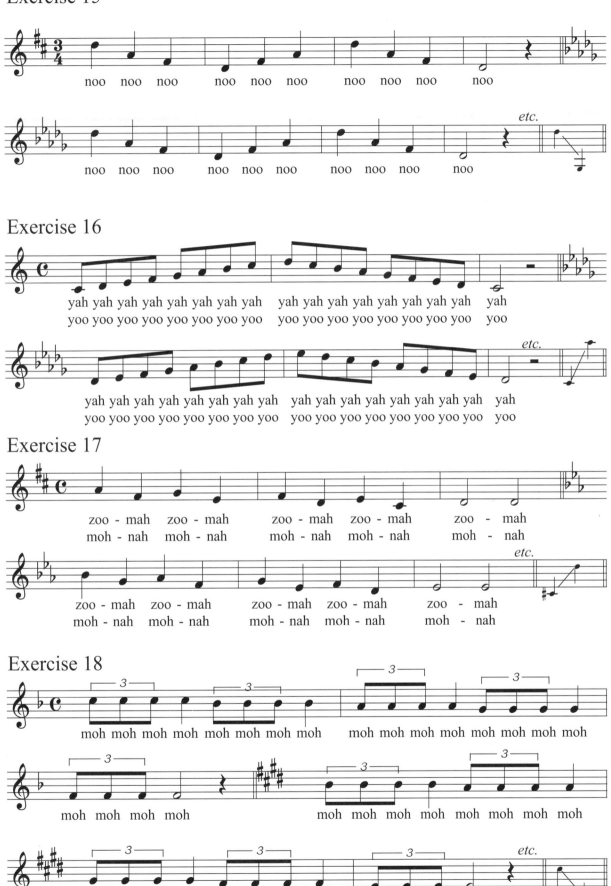

Exercise 16

Exercise 17

Exercise 18

Exercise 19

mah - mah - mee - ah   mah - mah - mee - ah   mah - mah - mee - ah   mah

mah - mah - mee - ah   mah - mah - mee - ah   mah - mah - mee - ah   mah

Exercise 20

nah_____   noh_____   nah_____   noh_____   nah

nah_____   noh_____   nah_____   noh_____   nah

Exercise 21

noo____   noo____   noo____   noo____   noo____   noo

noo____   noo____   noo____   noo____   noo____   noo

Exercise 22

nah____   noh____   nah____   noh____   nah____   noh____   nah____   noh

nah____   noh____   nah____   noh____   nah____   noh____   nah____   noh

11. Exercises for loosening and activating the lips

The lips form sounds just as the hands of a potter form clay. They are indispensable for the texture and formation of vowels and act as a "horn" or "bell" for our voice. Singers often have stiff lips, jutting lower lips or stretched lips. The following exercises loosen up the lips and make them supple.

Exercise 1

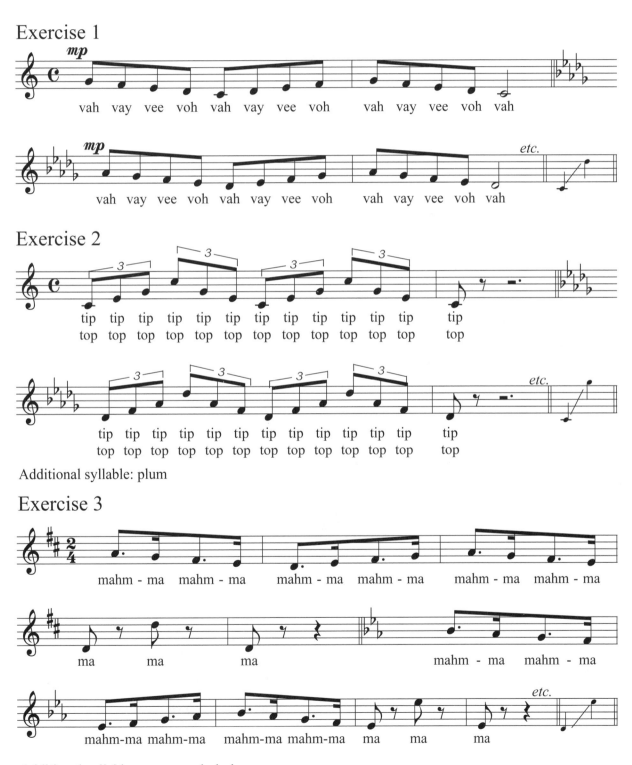

Additional syllable: plum

Exercise 3

Additional syllables: noo-noo, lo lo lo

Exercise 4

vee-loh-ray-see   vee-loh-ray-see   vee-loh-ray-see   vee-loh-ray-see   vah   vah   vah

vee-loh-ray-see   vee-loh-ray-see   vee-loh-ray-see   vee-loh-ray-see   vah   vah   vah

Exercise 5

vee vah vee vah vee vah   vee vah vee vah vee vah   vee   vah___

vee vah vee vah vee vah   vee vah vee vah vee vah   vee   vah___

Exercise 6

noo noo noo noo noo noo noo noo   noo noo noo noo noo
loh loh loh loh loh loh loh loh   loh loh loh loh loh

noo noo noo noo noo noo noo noo   noo noo noo noo noo
loh loh loh loh loh loh loh loh   loh loh loh loh loh

Exercise 7

vah vay vee vah vay vee vah vay vee vah vay vee vah vay vee vah vay vee vah vay vee vah

52

12. Exercises in Dynamics

Correctly interpreted dynamics, such as *crescendo – decrescendo* or *piano* and *forte*, are what give music its richness and colour. Unfortunately, choruses and soloists often sing *crescendi* like this: ▬◁▭ instead of this ◁▬. Many choruses have difficulty singing quietly. The tone becomes breathy, because poor vocal cord closure allows unused air to escape.

Exercise 1*

nah   nah   nah nah nah nah nah nah nah_____

nah   nah   nah nah nah nah nah nah nah_____   *etc.*

*This exercise is also suitable for warming up in the low range

Exercise 2

We   sing,   we   sing,   we   sing._____
We   sang,   we   sang,   we   sang._____
We   sung,   we   sung,   we   sung._____

We   sing,   we   sing,   we   sing._____   *etc.*
We   sang,   we   sang,   we   sang._____
We   sung,   we   sung,   we   sung._____

Additional syllables: we drive, we drove

Exercise 3

nah nah nah   nah_____   nah nah nah nah nah nah   nah
noh noh noh   noh_____   noh noh noh noh noh noh   noh

nah nah nah   nah_____   nah nah nah nah nah nah   nah   *up or down*
noh noh noh   noh_____   noh noh noh noh noh noh   noh

Exercise 4

noh noh noh noh noh noh
yoo yoo yoo yoo yoo yoo
zah zah zah zah zah zah

noh noh noh noh noh noh
yoo yoo yoo yoo yoo yoo
zah zah zah zah zah zah

Exercise 5

nah nah nah nah   nah nah nah nah   nah nah

nah nah nah nah   nah nah nah nah   nah nah

Exercise 6

noh   noh   noh
zah   zah   zah

Exercise 7

nah nah nah nah   nah nah nah nah   nah
noh noh noh noh   noh noh noh noh   noh

A dynamics exercise in combination with ear training

13. Warm-up exercises combined with ear training

Warm-up exercises that involve the singing of intervals also train a choral singer's ear. They should not be sung too loudly and the singer should inwardly "hear" each interval before singing it. Clear intonation requires continuous matching of the voice to the instrument (am I too high or too low?). However, this is not only a question of ear training, but also depends on whether a tone is produced correctly from the outset. Good singing technique usually solves intonation problems automatically.

Exercise 1

This exercise can also be sung legato.

Exercise 2

Exercise 3

hah hah hah hah hah hah hah hah hah

hah hah hah hah hah hah hah hah hah

Always inwardly "hear" the new key before singing it. Sing without an accompanying instrument.

Exercise 4

nah nah nah nah nah nah nah nah nah nah

nah nah nah nah nah nah nah nah nah nah

Exercise 5

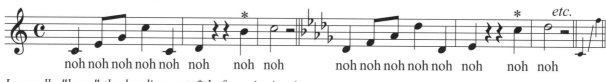

noh noh noh noh noh noh noh noh noh noh noh noh noh noh noh noh

Inwardly "hear" the leading note* before singing it.

Exercise 6

nah nah nah nah nah nah nah nah nah nah nah nah nah nah nah nah

*See footnote to Exercise 5.

Exercise 7

nah nah nah nah nah nah nah nah nah nah nah nah nah nah nah nah nah nah

Exercise 8

zoh zoh zoh zoh zoh zoh zoh zoh zoh zoh zoh zoh zoh

zoh zoh zoh zoh zoh zoh zoh zoh zoh zoh zoh zoh zoh

Exercise 9

noh noh noh noh noh noh noh noh noh noh noh noh noh

noh noh noh noh noh noh noh noh noh noh noh noh noh

Exercise 10

nah nah nah nah nah nah nah nah nah nah nah nah nah nah nah

nah nah nah nah nah nah nah nah nah nah nah nah nah nah nah

Exercise 11

nah nah nah nah nah nah nah nah nah nah

nah nah nah nah nah nah nah nah nah nah

Exercise 12

noh noh noh noh noh noh noh noh noh noh

noh noh noh noh noh noh noh noh noh noh

Exercise 13

oo_____ oh_____ ah_____

oo_____ oh_____ ah_____ *etc.*

Exercise 14

oo_____ oh_____ ah_____

oo_____ oh_____ ah_____ *etc.*

Exercise 15

nah nah nah nah nah nah nah nah nah nah nah

nah nah nah nah nah nah nah nah nah nah nah *etc.*

Exercise 16

Soprano/Alto

yo yo yo yo yo yo yo yo yo yo yo yo yo yo yo yo yo yo yo yo yo
yah yah yah yah yah yah yah yah yah yah yah yah yah yah yah yah yah yah yah yah yah

Tenor/Bass

yo yo yo yo yo yo yo yo yo yo yo yo yo yo yo yo yo yo yo yo yo *etc.*
yah yah yah yah yah yah yah yah yah yah yah yah yah yah yah yah yah yah yah yah yah

14. Warm-up exercises combined with exercises for developing a sense of rhythm

Modern song music needs a "groove", without which it lacks the right feeling. While it is important to sing with raw emotion, a detailed mathematical command of rhythm is a basic prerequisite for getting the right groove. In addition to warming up, the following exercises are intended to help develop a mastery of rhythm.

Exercise 5

tah tah___ tah   tah tah   tah   tah   tah tah___ tah
dah dah___ dah   dah dah___ dah   dah   dah dah___ dah

tah tah___ tah   tah   tah tah___ tah   tah tah___ tah   tah
dah dah___ dah   dah   dah dah___ dah   dah dah___ dah   dah

Exercise 6

nah nah___ nah nah   nah   nah nah___ nah nah   nah

Exercise 7

noh noh noh___ noh___ noh   noh   noh noh noh___ noh___ noh   noh

noh noh noh___ noh___ noh   noh   noh noh noh___ noh___ noh   noh

Exercise 8

zoh zoh   zoh zoh zoh_____   zoh zoh   zoh zoh zoh_____

Exercise 9

tah tah___ tah___   tah tah___ tah___   tah tah___ tah___

60

Exercise 10

tah tah tah___ tah tah___ tah___ tah___ tah___ tah___

tah tah tah___ tah tah___ tah___ tah___ tah___ tah___

Exercise 11

nah nah nah___ nah___ nah nah nah nah___ nah___ nah nah

nah nah nah___ nah___ nah nah nah nah___ nah___ nah nah

Exercise 12

tah tah tah___ tah___ tah tah tah tah___ tah___ tah tah

tah tah tah___ tah___ tah tah tah tah___ tah___ tah tah

Exercise 13

nah nah nah nah___ nah nah nah nah nah nah nah nah nah nah___ nah nah nah___nah_

nah nah nah nah___ nah nah nah nah nah nah nah nah nah nah___ nah nah nah___nah_

Exercise 14

Refrain of the black spiritual song "I'm Gonna Ride In The Chariot"

Exercise 15

Exercise 16

tah tah tah tah___ tah___ tah   tah tah tah tah___

tah tah tah tah___ tah___ tah   tah tah tah tah___

etc.

Exercise 17

nah nah nah nah___ nah nah nah nah_ nah nah nah nah nah nah _ nah_ nah nah nah nah_

nah nah nah nah___ nah nah nah nah_ nah nah nah nah nah nah _ nah_ nah nah nah nah_

etc.

Exercise 18

nah nah nah___ nah___ nah_____   nah nah nah___ nah___ na_____

simile

nah nah nah___ nah___ nah_____   nah nah nah___ nah___ nah_____

nah nah nah___ nah___ nah_____   nah nah nah___ nah___ nah_____

etc.

Exercise 19

noh noh noh___ noh noh noh noh   noh noh noh___ noh noh noh noh

noh noh noh___ noh noh noh noh   noh noh noh___ noh noh noh noh

etc.

15. Suggestions for accompaniment and performance

What is the best way to lead a chorus or soloist through the exercises? The following options exist:

1. Lead off by humming the first note or playing the first chord on a keyboard instrument. Then give the chorus the signal to begin. After each sequence, give the first note again, maintaining the specified rhythm throughout the exercise. In this way you give the singers momentum and motivation. In addition, the chorus singers or soloists can check with the keyboard instrument to find out whether they are staying in tune.

Example 1

Example 2

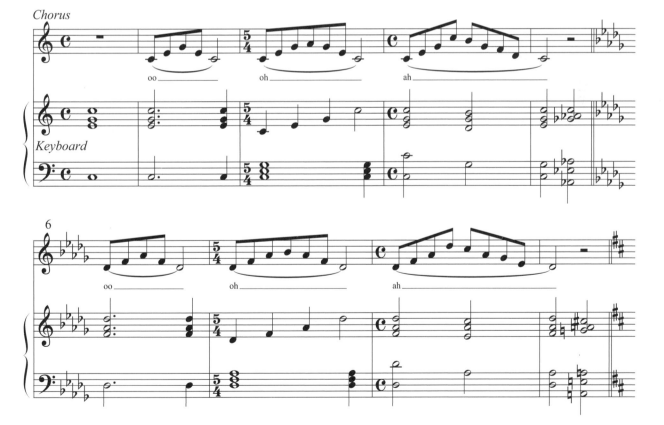

2. Play only the first note or chord. The chorus or soloist should then find the next starting note on its/his own (e.g. a semitone higher). It takes longer to get accustomed to this type of singing. It combines warm-up exercises with ear training and is therefore very effective.

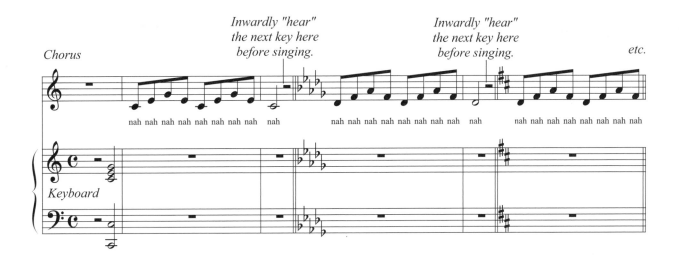

Helmut Barbe
Drei Nachtstücke
(Li-Tai-Pe/Klabund)
SSAATTBB • SKR 20503

Hans-Jürgen von Bose
Karfreitags-Sonett
(Andreas Gryphius)
SATB • SKR 20016
Todesfuge (Paul Celan)
SSAATTBB mit Bariton-Solo
und Orgel • SKR 20022
Vier Madrigale aus
„Die Leiden des jungen
Werthers"
SSATB • SKR 20015

Claude Debussy
Trois Chansons de Charles
d'Orléans
SATB • SKR 19006

Petr Eben
– *Psalmi peregrini* (Bibel)
SATB • SKR 20043
Verba sapientiae
SATB
– *De circuitu aeterno*
(Liber Ecclesiastes)
SKR 20026
– *Laus mulieris* (Liber
Proverbiorum)
SKR 20027
– *De tempore* (Liber Ecclesiastes)
SKR 20025

Jean Françaix
Trois Poëmes de Paul Valéry
SSAATTBB • SKR 20008

Hans Werner Henze
Hirtenlieder aus der Oper
„Venus und Adonis"
(Hans-Ulrich Treichel)
SMezATBarB • SKR 20046
Orpheus Behind the Wire
(Edward Bond)
SSSAAATTTBBB • SKR 20007

Kurt Hessenberg
Christus, der uns selig macht,
op. 118 (Michael Weiße)
SSATBB • SKR 20017
Psalm 130, op. 134
SATB • SKR 20024
Tröstet mein Volk, op. 114
(Jesaja 40, Erasmus Alber)
SSATBB • SKR 20005

Paul Hindemith
Zwölf Madrigale
(Josef Weinheber)
SSATB
Heft 1 Nr. 1-4 • SKR 20031
Heft 2 Nr. 5-7 • SKR 20032
Heft 3 Nr. 8-9 • SKR 20033
Heft 4 Nr. 10-12 • SKR 20034

Wilhelm Killmayer
Sonntagsgeschichten (Killmayer)
SATB
– *Sonntagsausflug*
SKR 20013
– *Sonntagsgedanken*
SKR 20014
– *Sonntagsnachmittagskaffee*
SKR 20004
Vier Chorstücke
SATB mit Soli (SATB)
SKR 20029

György Ligeti
Drei Phantasien
(Friedrich Hölderlin)
SSSSAAAATTTTBBBB
SKR 20003
Magány (Sándor Weöres)
SABar • SKR 20019
Magyar Etüdök (Sándor Weöres)
SSSSAAAATTTTBBBB
SKR 20006
Pápainé (ung. Volksballade)
SATB • SKR 20018

Krzysztof Penderecki
Agnus Dei (Ordinarium Missae)
SSAATTBB • SKR 20002
Cherubinischer Lobgesang
(russische Liturgie)
SSAATTBB • SKR 20020
De profundis (Psalm 129,1-5)
SATB/SATB/SATB • SKR 20039
Veni creator (Hrabanus Maurus)
SSAATTBB • SKR 20021

Heinrich Poos
Epistolae (Bibel, Martin Luther)
SSSAAATTTBBB mit Soli (SSSA)
SKR 20041
Hypostasis vel Somnium Jacob
(Bibel)
SSATBB • SKR 20035
Orpheus' Laute
(William Shakespeare)
SSATB/SSATB • SKR 20044
Sphragis (Ovid, altfranzösisches
Chanson)
SSATBB • SKR 20009

Aribert Reimann
Auf verschleierten Schaukeln
(Hans Arp)
SATB • SKR 20010
Nunc dimittis (Canticum
Simeonis)
SSAATTBB mit Bariton-Solo
und Bassflöte • SKR 20504

Christian Ridil
Nachts (Horst Lange)
SSAATTBB • SKR 20001

Dieter Schnebel
Amazones (Heinrich von Kleist)
SSMezAA • SKR 20038
Motetus
SATB/SATB • SKR 20028

Arnold Schönberg
Dreimal tausend Jahre, op. 50 A
(Dagobert D. Runes)
SATB • SKR 19007
Friede auf Erden, op. 13
(C. F. Meyer)
SSAATTBB • SKR 19008

Rodion Shchedrin
Concertino
SATB • SKR 20040

Wolfgang Steffen
Tagnachtlied, op. 50
(Lothar Klünner)
SSSSAAATTTBBBB • SKR 20502

Pēteris Vasks
Litene (Uldis Berzins)
SSSSAAATTTBBBB • SKR 20030
Three Poems by Czeslaw Milosz
ATTB • SKR 20036
Zemgale (Mara Zalite)
SSSSAAATTTBBBB • SKR 20037

Roland Willmann
Nox et tenebrae et nubila
(Aurelius Prudentius)
SSAATTBB • SKR 20501